THINKING OF
HAPPINESS

Thinking of Happiness

MICHAEL LASKEY

PETERLOO POETS

First published in 1991
by Peterloo Poets
2 Kelly Gardens, Calstock, Cornwall PL18 9SA, U.K.

© 1991 by Michael Laskey

**A catalogue record for this book is available
from the British Library**

ISBN 1-871471-23-0

Printed in Great Britain by
Latimer Trend & Company Ltd, Plymouth

ACKNOWLEDGEMENTS are due to the editors of the following journals and anthologies where these poems first appeared: *Argo, Arvon/Observer Prizewinners' Anthologies '85* and *'87, Belfast Review, The Cricketer, Encounter, Foolscap, Grand Piano, The Green Book, Harry's Hand, Illuminations, Iron, Literary Review, London Magazine, Other Poetry, Poetry Durham, Poetry Review, Rhinoceros, The Rialto, The Spectator, Stand, Thames Poetry, Times Literary Supplement* and *Verse.*

'Couplets for the Twins' was broadcast on *Poetry Now* on BBC Radio 3 and 'A Late Wedding Anniversary Poem' and 'Between Two Lit Rooms' on *Pen to Paper*, Radio 4.

'Cucumber' and 'Cloves of Garlic' were previously included in a short collection called *Cloves of Garlic* which was published by Smith Doorstep in 1989, being the joint winner of the 1988 Poetry Business Pamphlet Competition.

This volume was published with assistance from the Ralph Lewis Award at the University of Sussex.

Supported by

Cornwall
County Council

WITH THE ASSISTANCE OF

SOUTH WEST ARTS

Recipient of an Arts Council Incentive Funding Award

for
Ben, Tim and Jack

Contents

page

9 Stills

12 A Curse on the Editors of Poetry Review

14 On the Anniversary of V.E. Day 1985

15 Meeting our Father

16 Letters from my Mother

17 Couplets for the Twins

18 Fishing for Mackerel

20 The Enclosure

22 A Change of Clothes

23 A Charm for Maurice

24 The Waitress

25 In Defence of the N.H.S.

26 Honouring a Debt

27 The Fancy

29 Photographs

30 A Tray of Eggs

31 Weekends

32 Firelighters

33 Between Two Lit Rooms

34 Bedtime Songs

35 Family Planning

36 A Late Wedding Anniversary Poem

37 Registers

38 Solidarity with Seven-Year-Olds

39 Pater Familias

41 Living with the Doctor

43 On Having Given Up Cricket

44 On the A12

45 Living with a Death

48 Recognitions

49 Sea-Anglers

50 Laying the Fire

51 In Another Country
52 Sleep-Talking
53 In Aldringham Churchyard, Suffolk
54 Herring
57 On the Roderigo (H135) lost with all hands in 1955
58 The New People
59 Life after Death
60 Cucumber
61 Mourning
62 Cloves of Garlic

Stills

The silence of five hundred boys
in the hall is vibrant with noise,
as the hymn they're about to sing
will end up being sort of sung.

**

The boys are writing. Their glances
rest on him briefly, not seeing
how this is anywhere, any time,
how he could be D.H. Lawrence.

**

We can't take our eyes off the high
ball, the break well spent studying
perfect parabolas, hanging on
for the next uncertain catch.

**

Today the growth of trade unions,
Mr Beacom dictating his honed
notes to the fifth year. They're writing
machines, with their minds idling.

**

In the chemi lab a simple
experiment: iron and sulphur
compounded will glow red hot;
Vaughan will call Wetherby 'Bob'.

**

These boys stand as mute as the carved
desk-lid one of them grips. Their guilt,
their fear hurts. At the door Porky
is waiting for an explanation.

**

The ding-dong dining hall jangle
and tall talk suddenly dwindle:
we titter a little or grin,
abashed by the angel passing.

**

Pandemonium in R.I.
again. The Reverend Argylle
turns on a harmless boy who stops
laughing. He won't be forgotten.

**

At the afternoon's darkest point
a boy starts to feel, to work
his way to a thought. Oblivious
of us and that look on his face.

**

Once through the main doors he's struck
by the smell, the distant tumult:
despite his black bag and his grey
Volvo he's new and knows nothing.

**

From here you can see top field
enlivened by blue and white boys
moving between line-out and scrum,
but you need to supply your own sounds.

**

In one class what a diversity
of noises, raised voices, faces
turning to the teacher briefly:
he's losing faith in his mark-book.

**

When the bell, shrilling for the end
of last period, stops and before
the first boys come booming out
into the corridor, that's when.

**

For those coming after he leaves
an orderly form-room, the chairs
on the desks with their legs in the air
till tomorrow or forever.

**

A child running towards us falls.
We watch him raise his head and hold
our breath. His mouth is a gaping
hole of silence filling us all.

A Curse on the Editors of Poetry Review

Young hawks of English Literature
I do not doubt that now you soar
your stoop will be spectacular,
your quarry choice, your judgement sure—
by now it should be quite mature.

Young Mick Imlah and Tracey Warr,
for six months I've been waiting for
your verdict on my modest four
poems posted through your door
at Earls Court Square.

Meanwhile the summer package tours
have left the sea to wash the shore;
the squirrel has mislaid his store;
the hawthorn has achieved the haw;
our leaning snowman feels the thaw

and I, who for so long forbore
complaint, invoke the voice of Thor
to terrorise you to the core
with iron curses I forswore
till Mick Imlah and Tracey Warr.

For every poem you ignore
may you attract a further score,
each one more vexingly obscure
and either brilliant or a bore—
may you grow daily more unsure.

May all the poems you've crammed in drawers
conspire to form a lovesick corps
of adolescent troubadours
to caterwaul from nine to four
each working day outside your door.

And may your friends and any whore
whom you frequent to ease your sore
heads jangled by freak metaphors
discover their vocation for
comic verse you must endure.

And may your dreams be shifting floors
of manuscripts with massive claws
and raw brains dangling from their jaws
so you will scream and wake and gnaw
your nail moons while poets snore.

And though you write letters galore
of resignation, you too, Warr,
will find your manuscripts ignored.
And Imlah, *your* fate will be similar,
interminably half an editor.

I'm almost sorry for you, poor
hopeless Imlah, desperate Warr.

On the Anniversary of V.E. Day 1985

After the speeches, the solemn faces,
the muted melancholic brass,
once more silence.

I still don't know what my father thought
feeling his Lancaster lifting off
into the huge cockpit of night.

Or Uncle Len, injured, I know
only by hearsay, at Mount Cassino—
the wound didn't show.

They both survived to find me fat
on my mother's lap. Killers,
victims, my first real men.

But they wouldn't speak of what they'd done
or had done to them;
they held their peace

and hold it still,
remarkable as this pill-box standing
out in the currents of corn.

Meeting our Father

Almost unbearable having to wait
and wait in the terminal building
checking all-comers. A year it had been—
his job, mum said—but we knew him at once—
his features varnished—and raced to be first
at his side and allowed to uncover the budgie:
a fearful clatter of wings. Lupin.
Not used to us yet. And though we began
teaching him carols on the way home,
his cage balanced on our bare knees,
we soon went quiet, seeing how silly
our hopes had been. And he never spoke,
though he'd settle on my head while I did my prep
and lived with us years after Dad had left.

Letters from my Mother

Roughly once a month
in prompt response to mine
her envelopes arrive:

loyal to her brand
of stationery, her firm
rounded hand unchanged.

Through my unsettled years
of doors she never saw
and views she couldn't share

she's kept it up, composed
God only knows what quires
of cheerful humdrum prose.

Like this one, bland with facts,
with golf, gardening, weather
and names of those who came:

eight sides of unevent-
ful life with what went on
inside her head left out

as if of no account.
The same dear selfless door.
No hint that she's afraid
it's cancer.

Couplets for the Twins

2.2.1986

Without pushing, with no palaver
having made room for one another

in the same womb, you're still together
at seventy, as close as ever:

the tick and tock of the same clock,
the intimate click of key and lock,

the struck match and your sizzling laughter
still rocketing off even after

the years of those other more urgent bonds—
husbands and children—have come and gone.

Separate journeys, but never apart:
shadowed by an unobtrusive thought;

or a mirror missed from the entrance hall,
its negative image bleached on the wall.

Faces as teasing as tongue twisters.
Grace lavished on us in twin sisters:

at your double birth a sudden thaw
in the frozen core of the first world war,

your moist mouths softening the air,
your cries cutting cleanly through barbed wire;

and through our grim century these twin
premises and grounds for optimism.

Fishing for Mackerel

for Mike Curtis

On all that wide water he and I
dispersed along flightpaths of birds flocking
across the unfenced fields of sky
and we wheeled freely back to the rocking
boat with its wake running straight to Cley
and our talk overlapping, interlocking,

till at length I asked 'Where's the rod and reel?
And what bait do they take, these mackerel?'
and Curt, startled by my revealed
ignorance, drew from the cluttered well
of the boat hand-lines which he unpeeled,
each one barbed at tactical

intervals with a dozen steel
hooks and vividly coloured feathers:
fast food with mackerel appeal.
So we dropped our lines down into that nether
world looming up underneath our keel
and sat back to wait together.

And if I was sceptical, if I was never
to catch a mackerel, what the hell?
If this was fishing, then no endeavour
had ever suited me half as well,
with half a mind on the hand's light tether
riding with Curt on the slow sea swell,

till this spell of content tensed, shattered
at a yank from below, a simultaneous yell
of delight from Curt as the shoal battered
by and we gathered our catch up into the bell
of the air, their tails gonging like clappers,
immaculate, miraculous mackerel:

not one at a time, but four or five
jangling my line, as the shoal without number
or interruption still arrived
and, while I was fumbling, would have passed under
our bows and vanished, had not Curt, alive
to my flapping, expertly unencumbered

his line and mine and flung them back
and, before I'd even half-grasped my luck
or my thankfulness, more fish snatched
at our hooks; and although we must have struck
and singled them out, yet we too were their catch,
clutched by their bubbling life bursting up.

When I think of happiness, I think of that.

The Enclosure

Walking here
in was it March
we saw the roped off
length of beach,
read the notice
out and laughed,
it just seemed daft.

But back in June
passing between
the tide line
and the line of stakes,
still only linked
by one slack strand
of baler twine,

above the din
of wind and waves
and pebbles grating
under feet,
we heard the sharp
repeated peep
of an alarmed

little tern
flying over
the enclosure,
its fearful threats
alerting us
to eggs here somewhere
on the shingle.

And as we looked
around more birds
materialised,
more terns with slim
decisive wings:
the quick of clouds
secured by string.

A Change of Clothes

Always I knew there'd been knitted rugs
pat on the lino in my parents' room:
punts to push off on or stepping stones
I could change on a whim, to frighten myself,
into crocodiles. The cane-seated chair
had always been there, right-angled, handily
placed for my climb up the bed's sheer face
and onto the plateau of Saturday morning,
when the world moved over and let me in.
There under the Heath, next door to the station—
Gospel Oak—and close to the shops
at South End Green, what more could I want?

Not school—not learning my name was odd;
or having Steve Lawrence ask why my Dad
and Mum spoke funny; or under their bed
one wet afternoon finding the case
carefully packed: a change of clothes
even for me, some papers in English
and some in a language that had to be Polish,
and right at the bottom a wallet containing
£25 that over the years,
needing this and that, I gradually spent,
each time really meaning to pay it all back.

A Charm for Maurice

Only just arrived, only just alive,
a bare kilo for special care,
premature baby boy grown man
in more minds than mine, gramme by gramme
add weight to hopes we hardly dare
breathe for a future where you'll thrive

unfussed, unfêted, undiscussed
for days on end, where you can sleep
heavily in your room next door
to Graham and Tanya, or peel and core
their apple of sleep with your most sweet
incisive cries—if you must.

But now in an incubator, fed through the nose,
shielded by perspex, by nurses, by prayer,
Thursday's child, with so far to go
to wear your folded baby clothes,
journey to the threshold of fresh air,
outgrowing this poem and putting on prose.

The Waitress

by Manet

She's loading up at the bar
sideways on, between customers,
her eyes caught remembering where
she's going, who these beers are for.

All evening, steadily, she bears
full glasses to tables and returns
with dead ones, with orders for more.
Her hand through the beer's blurred.

On the stage behind her some song
or dance routine's going on:
a redhead's spreading bare arms,
bare shoulders lifting the tune

musicians are playing at her feet.
All eyes are on the artiste—
a blue sash clasping her waist,
her dress a sway of white lace—

and only la servante de bocks
faces this way, dressed in black
with a white frill of blouse at the neck,
white apron, her sleeve folded back.

In the thick of things, but so still
that suddenly she's visible
and we know her, she's that nice girl
married to old thingummy from Lille.

In Defence of the N.H.S.

In certain parts of South America 'half of private patients have cæsarean sections, and operation rates are directly related to the woman's income and inversely related to her degree of risk.'
Marion H. Hall, BMJ Vol. 294. 24.1.87

It's five in the afternoon.
Exactly five o'clock—
the cathedral carillon chiming—
as the doctor, Don Ramón Echevarría,
enters the gleaming theatre
in the Queen of Heaven Clinic,
putting an end to ease.

The anæsthetist tightens a final nozzle,
masked nurses and junior doctors
back off, open a path to the table
where la Señora Carrera Velarde
is breathing oxygen and expecting
her first baby by cæsarean section
this afternoon.

You can tell by her perfectly manicured nails,
by the gloss on her skin, her soft hair,
that she'll never know labour;

though all her babies, fat jugs lined up,
would tip themselves naturally into the cup
of the cervix without his expertise.

So I don't want to see it,
I don't want to watch the incision
the doctor is making, his sharp
practice, his dark red Mercedes
reversing in the hospital car park.

Honouring a Debt

       Knowing this:
that the mother beside the frozen foods
smacking her son to stop him crying
from the pain of her grip and jerk on the chain

       of his arm
did me good. Better than a paragon
of parenthood, firmed up my tenderness.
One by one I touched my sons.

       Bless you
mother, at the check-out, shame-faced,
the clench and wrench of your anger spent,
ignorant of my indebtedness.

The Fancy

Glanced out this lunchtime and saw old Threadkell
coming home, his rusty blue van
turning into the lane opposite,
a neighbour of mine I consider
      hardly at all;

as he'll still walk by me not meeting
my eye, not even slightly inclining
his head. But whether he disapproves
of me particularly or would withhold
      recognition

indifferently from anyone living
opposite him for a mere six years
I don't know. Perfect love would be to care
for him like air, enlivening the brick
      wall of his face

unnoticed, without ulterior motives.
Imperfectly I try to imagine
I'm an unsmiling, early rising, gruff,
tough, retired agricultural worker
      and widower

like Jack Threadkell, wedded to a treadmill
of practical tasks: tending slow vegetables;
cooped up with hens and the more unlikely
sprightly bantams he breeds for the fancy;
      then off somewhere

with his chain-saw slung in the back of the van
among the muscular clutter of tools
he knows how to use. And now home for dinner.
I watch him drive in, hear the engine die,
      the van-door slam.

Staring out blankly I feel my features
worked quickly, reshaped to fit a new face:
it's his dead wife seizing her chance to peer
out through my eyes, soothed to catch sight of him
          looking so well.

Photographs

Everything belongs to everything
this afternoon. The ice, which has soldered
streams, secret creeks and welded
the lake waters, holds us, is holding,
so speech between strangers is simple.

This greybeard's a boy again skating
and in turn boys are recklessly sliding
their shadows' length, absently filing
raw air, red sunlight, compiling
the fabulous winters of childhood.

Only Leo I notice is separate,
on the landing stage, burdened with a foolish
camera, stamping cold feet.
A novice, a father who belongs
to his daughters now only on Sundays.

A Tray of Eggs

It's not the hens that matter,
scratching among the nettle
roots at the orchard's edge,
though much might be made of their red
foppish cockscombs, their speckled
feathers overlapping and the stutter
of their daft, deft pecking.

Nor is it the road pedalled
by heart to the farm, the known
fields never the same,
turning from a greenness to grain,
revolving, resolving into rows
of straight seedlings, stubble
burnt or interred under furrows.

Not even the ride shared
with my two-year-old child, astride
the crossbar, breathing the blown
scents he's making his own
unknowingly, being alive
to vibrations of place this admired
Ford tractor amplifies.

But what counts more than these small
pleasures are the eggs we bring home
in boxes and softly transpose
into the bevelled holes
in the cardboard tray, the domes
of these thirty shells
that will break like the days to come.

Weekends

for Ben Horwood at forty

Returning your Joe, at what would have been dusk
but for the snow: with a one-track mind
on the tight-rope road, driving slowly

and, despite packed ice and Joe's distracting
narrative eccentricities, we
arrived at the gate as you stepped out:

not content with an afternoon spent
skating, but now going, racing the dark,
up Bramblebush with the older two

for a quick sledge, pulling behind you
The Flexible Flyer—wood and metal
fast together these forty years.

I turned and drove alone through the given
weather, steadied by the thought of you, Ben,
plunging down into Sunday's last hollow.

Firelighters

for Lesley

Soon after he left you, another first:
entering the cold husk of the house
with two tired children you know the worst
has happened, the Parkray has gone out

and find yourself kneeling without thinking
without faith before the boiler,
riddling briskly, cinders and clinker
cleared, the grate a waiting void

which he'd have filled with his unhurried
origami, a fan of spills
pinched round compact coils and buried
under kindling, chips of coal.

Always miraculous that phoenix,
now extinguished. But all you need's
to hand: a screwed up man-size Kleenex,
a firelighter, some sticks and a hod

of coal to feed a single match.
Nothing to it. You lift the flap
for draught, adjust the thermostat
and feel warmth slowly welling up.

Between Two Lit Rooms

After work, for once, to walk home,
not to drive, foot hinged to the clutch,
through town, but to walk on your own
out into the open dark,

the Plough, the Pole Star, Orion
distancing you from your day.
Then down the ringing wrought-iron
spiral staircase to the softer

asphalt of the all but empty
car park. One January night.
Such space around you, such plenty:
a good fifteen minutes walking

between two lit rooms, the split halves
of your life, the future, the past.
But for now a skive down this path,
the ridge of the fence furred with frost.

Bedtime Songs

Ten years stretched out along-
side boys or stroking their small
heads through the bars of the cot
and every night wondering which
song to pin my voice on.

So many memorable songs
forlorn in the dark of my brain,
so few on the tip of my tongue,
that singing them's often no more
than routine, a stale refrain.

And yet I sing stubbornly on
settling my youngest son,
till suddenly, crying from her deep
sleep in my skull, here comes
Molly Malone with fresh fish.

Family Planning

We called you Jenny after the girl
who kissed Leigh Hunt, at once foresaw
how soon I'd bore you with his poem.

But after all you'll never know it:
no more children, we've agreed—
both being free and forced to choose.

Your three brothers, who brushed in turn
past your inapplicable name,
must go on growing up alone:

unmoved by the pull of their own
new moon, unrocked by a small
tyrannical sister. Our Jenny.

Nothing but a word; familiar
features resolutely blurred;
but the lips ineffably soft.

A Late Wedding Anniversary Poem

Knowing time's short in the rush
hour of breakfasts with children to crush
into coats and partings to brush

I tucked your second best bra
in over the radiator

so that hurrying to dress
you might almost feel me press
a warm hand around each breast.

Registers

Out of the warm primordial cave
of our conversations, Jack's gone.
No more chit-chat under the blankets
pegged over chairs and nipped in drawers.

Throughout his first five years an ear
always open, at worst ajar,
I catch myself still listening out
for sounds of him in the sensible house

where nothing stirs but the washing machine
which clicks and churns. I'm loosening his arms
clasped round my neck, detaching myself
from his soft protracted kiss goodbye.

Good boy, diminishing down the long
corridors into the huge unknown
assembly hall, each word strange,
even his name on Miss Cracknell's tongue.

Solidarity with Seven-Year-Olds

What thought went into this plastic
helmet. What a ponderous weight
of calculation, time and wit
teamed up to make the package fit
    Tim's soft head.

This cold shell lined with white and yellow
foam rubber. Made in Taiwan and
containerised. One loaded word—
BURNER—emblazoned on the curved
    snap-on visor.

It longed for him through Mr Nunn's
cunning window, a still unsullied
brilliant blue, silver-studded,
lacking only an able-bodied
    boy with money

in the bank, a matching bike
and resolute against advice.
There was no choice, my solo voice
inaudible above the noise
    made by Raleigh.

Those streamlined dreams his B.M.X.
helmet failed to realise.
Capitalism, damn your eyes.
Pick on someone less unwise.
    Try me for size.

Pater Familias

This morning I'm an old-fashioned man
manifest on the garage roof:
a bonus to most routine
pedestrians and a light relief
to the dustman laid back at my feet.

And the upturned face of the place
looks like itself, but strange,
with the width of the hedge displayed
and below me the highly strung
washing-line, the road going on

unrolled like the new felt left
on the grass—as Ernie advised—
to settle in the sun while I lift
greynesses of old galvanised
nail-heads with pliers or a knife

and strip off the felt which the years
have so hardened and cracked that rain
tracks through, drips everywhere.
Back to the bare boards. They grin
up at me, impressed, my children,

exclaim at the parallel slits
of sunshine defining the planks.
I climb down over the water-butt
to measure and cut seven lengths
of felt with conviction, teeth clenched.

Then back up: tacking them, one
by one, in position; slubbed
brushloads of thick black bitumen
lap cement under each edge;
working upwards to end with the ridge.

The whole morning battened down tight,
proof against children and the shared
chores of our up-to-date life.
Tomorrow Kay's the car and I'm child care,
but today here she comes with a beer.

Living with the Doctor

Once a week I suppose, like a white
wash or my cauliflower bake,
somebody living here dies;

and even if you don't go,
if it's not your day on call
or if you're away, you'll know

in the end: the others will usually
say or someone'll send you a form
if it happens in hospital.

Sometimes you tell me, name names
you think may ring bells for me—Elsie
Fairweather, old Billy Sore—

and sometimes you don't: you come in
bearing dry clothes from the line
which you fold while I'm dishing up lunch.

But on days you need to make sense
of an accident or to relax
the grip of a grief, then we speak

of who and how, what you could do
to help. We've had to develop
a voice that can cope with death

properly, yet fit it in
over our bowls of soup,
before we're summoned to watch

Jack's magic or unsnarl Ben's maths.
Privileged knowledge for me—
a broadening, a warning—

but for you I'm not so sure
this morning, finding your clothes
in a heap on the bathroom floor

and knowing you must have been out
on a call in the night. The jabbing
phone; your questions; our duvet

closing behind you; your footsteps:
I slept through them all, insensible
even to your shivering return.

On Having Given Up Cricket

I shall play cricket in heaven
in return for the afternoons
gladly given to the other
pleasure of other's leisure.

I shall walk, without haste, to the wicket
and nod to the angels kitted
in their whites waiting to discern
the kind of batspirit I am.

And one stroke in heaven, one dream
of a cover drive will redeem
every meeting of bat
and ball I've done without.

And I'll bowl too, come on to bowl
leg-breaks with such control
of flight and slight changes of pace
that one over will efface

the faint regret I now feel.
But best of all I shall field:
alert in the heavenly deep,
beyond the boundary of sleep.

On the A12

Towards the end of a long drive home,
your nervous system subdued by pistons,
your children, gone through the quarrelsome

miles, mild now in the back of your mind,
and the road once more your own, the known
camber of a bend, horizons, signs

you read for the sake of their refreshed
welcoming names, not to tick them off,
Ufford, Hacheston, Campsey Ash.

And it's almost over, you're all but back
unpacking, when for a sudden split
second the road, that must know the make

and colour of your car and your number plate,
turns towards your returning smile
a quite blank unfamiliar face

so out of place you can't remember
where in the wheeling world you are
or what time it is of what day, month, year.

Living with a Death

for my wife's mother

1.
These ceremonies, Gee, to mark
your death, two hundred miles away
from us, though with your girls, today:

for Jack and me a sweet unique
after breakfast hour of sleep
that creased our clothes but soothed our souls;

between the sandpit and the swings
a comma in mid-afternoon,
its ragged wings in perfect tune;

to fetch the older boys from school
a borrowed dormobile, a slow
heightened ride round our known roads;

then sherry in your memory
and nuts they did their best to share
lovingly with you not here.

I think you know it all, our tears
and Ben and Tim asleep upstairs
for comfort in a single bed.

2.
What I remember best is this:
the wonderful heaviness of your head
on my shoulder where you'd fallen asleep
for the first time. Whatever was said
was as nothing to that.
                            Though all you meant
was a warm on the bed, a breather, a break
from the rigours of revision, the cold

45

afternoon laid the blankets of dusk
so imperceptibly over us

                              that you slept on
undisturbed and I, far too elated
to sleep, still shouldered the weight of your trust.

So tonight lay down your boulder of grief;
let it ache in the same old feeling place.

3.
On Thorpeness beach—where he saw her last,
and most, in the three light years their lives
overlapped—out for a walk,

a winter walk, our boots making blunt
dents in the pebbles, felicitous prints
in a narrow strip of blank new sand.

With her four months dead he hopes she still
remembers us. Leaving these tracks,
these vestiges on Thorpeness beach.

4.
Your face turned away into shadow:
your dead mother, dishevelled,
fossicking about in the cellar
after the Scrabble you casually
smuggled out, years back.

But pleased to be called up, released
from amnesia—those cobwebs,
the damp—she picks her fastidious
way up the steps and appears
in the doorway, the daylight, delighted

you've arrived. And now comes alive
receiving you, free to speak
again after weeks on her own,
excusing her hair, the dust
brushed off her skirt and the Scrabble

still inexplicably lost.
As she lists the places she's looked
we're nodding, our eyes not meeting,
not daring to speak, but shaking
with spasms of laughter and grief.

5.
In the deep night Jack cried out
and woke me. What was the matter?

Plainly from his dream he spoke:
'Gee's only got one cover.'

Gee, his eighteen-month-dead
grandmother.

I fetch him a drink and stroke
his snug five-year-old head.

Small wonder she wants to be heard,
mourned, not settled forever

under thick blankets of years.

Recognitions

In the dream I was dead, waiting
anxiously, slowly moving
from chair to chair down a long
tunnel of a room funnelling
us all to the door in the end
wall and through it for judgement.

And found myself in the playroom
facing familiar shelves full
of tatty good intentions
and, picking over the debris
on the green carpet, a dozen
shining separate children.

Not mine or friends of mine,
but known to me from the moment
they lifted their faces and focused
on me: friends' children seen
incidentally across a room,
benignly saluted, discounted.

And these children I'd never stirred
myself to love had become
my judges. It was not to be borne,
their gaze, their unbroken silence.
Tamsin, Tom, Jonathan, Gill...
I woke myself calling their names.

Sea-Anglers

Always there before us, green umbrellas
draw us to the anglers standing, arms crossed,
mindful of horizons and their rod-tips
but, beyond a nod, indifferent to our curious
clumping over pebbles through their silence.

Lost on them, our glance of admiration
at tackle-boxes trim in all compartments,
our eye caught by their bait: lug, undulant
and gleaming; on newspaper a mackerel
unfreezing, one flank sawn off down the backbone

with an old steel knife. Still life. We move on
down the beach. What are they hoping to catch?
Cod's what they'd say if pushed. And whiting, flats.
I can see one there quietly unscrewing
a thermos, imagine one lighting his lamp.

Laying the Fire

This is the way I deal with the news,
on my knees screwing up page after page
of the Guardians I hardly ever read
otherwise. To fill the grate it only takes
five double sheets, each one unpeeled
and crumpled up rapidly into a ball,
and, in between, time on my hands to read
anything eye-catching, headlines, this
girl of fourteen on a day return
from Durham, dazed by her concert, distressed
at not knowing which way to go for Kings Cross,
but not guessing, now she was guided by him,
how soon she'd be unforgettably lost.
Oh, as they were passing the door of his flat
they had to look in, he said, pick something up;
and once they were safely inside he wasted
no time: raped her, raped her, repeatedly
raped her until he lay limp, at last fell asleep
and she crept out through his open mouth
into the dark hollow of the street
needing help, healing, amnesia,
anger, but not this pair in a car cruising,
who caught her full in their lights—some wild
young slut appealing to them to stop,
asking for it. The end. That was the end
of the story. Another page screwed up,
paper ablaze, blackening, collapsing
under the weight of twigs, sticks, logs
laid in the hearth, gone up in smoke.

In Another Country

Some hold-up ahead, a toll perhaps or roadworks?
A checkpoint, soldiers, bored, with the usual
cradled rifles, one stiffly waving us forward

and you're smiling, winding down the window,
stirred, flushed by your knowledge of the language,
aiming an amiable patter of plosives

up at their faces, expecting some comeback,
a glittering crack of labials, gutturals,
not this sharpening, darkening silence. 'Ignorant

bastards' you growl, rolling the window
dismissively up, your fuming, your revving
cut short by the almost simultaneous

soldiers yanking at both back doors, collaring
the children, like cases, like carcasses,
lugging them off. Soundlessly screaming

I wake to the dark, our room, anguish
deeper than your breathing, and unrelieved
till a child—still alive—cries out for comfort:

It's only a dream, love, only a dream.

Sleep-Talking

Not the words it intrigues them to learn
they shouted out in their dreams—
Jack's pugnacity suddenly plainly
spoken—not that I mean,

but a voice so urgent, intense,
that the house, lightly holding its course
through darkness, is startled and turns
in on itself. Through doors

left ajar you're listening, disturbed
by what you've just heard, a child
somewhere forced to speak out, but in words
so garbled you'll never know why.

Only once. Then silence. The house,
slowly gathering momentum, starts breathing
more deeply. You lie back and doze,
or find your place, carry on reading.

In Aldringham Churchyard, Suffolk

Their flesh having failed to reach home,
only their names in alphabetical
order remain in memorial stone,

though in this uniform column of death
each individual's curt initials
stand for a life in civilian dress

before conscription, a breathing space
for Christian names, diminutives,
before the war they were made to make

prematurely struck them dumb:
one whose pilot misjudged a dive;
one whom a blind shell burst upon;

and another rolling a crafty fag
between fatigues, the simple sod,
crushed by a lorry a jaunty waaf

backed with panache to within an inch
of the wall he'd leant against, feeling good.
And though they died they left the skins

of their names behind and their frames of mind
to be used again by their next of kin
networking over these square miles:

Chandler, a fitter for Eastern Gas,
Church, a moonlighting handyman,
and Mower, bringing the milk through the dark.

Herring

Before he was fourteen my old man
shipped as cook with Ned Mullender
          on the *Fame*, I think,
out of Lowestoft for the home fishing,
          drifting for herring.

He learnt how to cook his beef pudding
and his plum duff, how to fry the herring—
          half a dozen each—
for breakfast and came to relish the rusks
          you had to soak

in brine to kill all the weevils off.
It was either that or the fish market.
          Herring was king
and any lad hardening in his service
          counted for something,

could wind up skipper, like my old boy,
after the years spent coiling the warp,
          hauling drenched nets,
swinging the quarter-cran baskets of herring
          onto the wharf,

fighting off sleep. In the dark so many
working Smiths Knoll, he'd blink sometimes,
          thinking it a fair-
sized town forward, not the fishing grounds.
          So dense with herring

that often the drifters coming in
had to moor not broadside along the quay
          but stem on, three deep,
and wait, wedged in thickets of rigging,
          sometimes half a day

with the silver herring still to scutch;
or they'd force open tenacious cracks,
            working the winch,
and screw themselves up through the barrage of boats
            and language, bucketfuls.

Troubled most by glut, by the market
depressed and fresh darlings to dump,
            they simply assumed
the herring was inexhaustible.
            Crass maybe,

but not greed. With us five kids to clothe
and feed, he was glad of the new purse-
            seine nets, his short
wave radio set and would have welcomed
            the echo-sounder

and the Decca navigator, if he'd lived.
The fleet vanished, efficiently steaming
            after the shimmer
of herring grown dimmer, thinned in the end
            by each advance;

and left him wildly, weakly threshing
in a net we smaller fry slipped through
            with no effort.
Now with a steady sou'westerly blowing
            and a full moon—

ideal for herring—I lie fifty
miles inland and listen to my wife
            breathing deeply.
She cries out once from a long way off,
            lost to my touch.

Tomorrow night, if I'm not too late,
and we can, we'll talk, tease at these black
      knots remembering
how, when they freed the cod-end, herring
      deluged the deck.

On the Roderigo (H135)
lost with all hands in 1955

Nothing but this rocking preposterous cradle
      between us and black water;
Iceland astern, a nuance, a nowhere.

All of us needed, subdued to our functions,
      knowing our value hangs on the trawl,
on the layers of dead cod boxed in the hold.

Then pitched into fear by an unforeseen fall
      in the temperature: spindrift, spray
not draining away but forming a skin,

calluses on deck, clinging to the rigging
      and the winch. Ice bracing itself
against the bridge, building up fast;

each swell, each squall driving more nails
      into our ever more top-heavy
cradle and coffin—only held up

by these numbskull axes perseveringly
      pecking away. No chance
of a smoke; not a hope of thanking

Ernie the cast off, who raised the alarm;
      or of needling George, the idle sod,
for once in his charmed life almost sweating.

The New People

won't stand for the stained scroll-footed bath
or the lack of double glazing;
will carpet our sometime varnished floorboards,
fill holes, drill holes, tap in rawl-plugs.
They'll annihilate our magnolia phase
with the new paints: a clap of cymbals.

I picture them settled before the fire,
before they've burnt all the leftover logs,
already feeling compatible, comfortable
coupling their names to the strange address,
attached to the post code. For they've succeeded
and we're superceded, we may well be dead.
But into their dreams of summer, of making
a start on the garden, we'll loose our swifts.

Life after Death

After he died he went on speaking
on the ansaphone: he'd apologise
for being out and ask us to leave
our names and messages after the tone.

At first we couldn't, we just hung up,
but steeled ourselves; it was her grief,
her tape that she was perfectly free
not to choose to erase in those early days.

At last though the voice did change to hers
and we were consoled, we found we could breathe
our nonsense into her solemn machine
once more and pictured her smiling, unwinding.

Later we raised it—macabre was the word
we used—and she laughed, told us the truth
was tougher, more matter of fact than that:
just not knowing how to record herself.

Cucumber

smiles on us too.
From its Latin root
cucumis creeps
through the centuries,
texture and taste
reaching us almost
unchanged, answering
to all but the same name.

Cucumber:
the levity of language
to settle on a word
so mimetic,
cylindrical
weighty and long,
of a ludicrous
bent like the fruit.

Cucumber:
a licence for staid
middle-aged men
out shopping,
like this one
prodding his son
in the back
with a cucumber gun.

Cucumber
cut for us, bleeds
minute plasma beads;
shows us its useless
rose windows,
its needless number
of seeds. Sixth proof
that God exists:

Cucumber.

Mourning

I bought a new pair of shoes
the day after hearing the news
of your death—

suddenly spendthrift, determined
to slop on no more on wet feet,
not mean for once with myself—

so I walk in the drizzle of grief
honouring you with dry feet
no less than those whose distress
is more formally expressed.

Cloves of Garlic

1.
The uncut pages of the garlic,
grained, white and inviting;
an uncertain number of cloves
feeling like a sequence of poems.

2.
'I am tired of the blandness of the world'
said God, as limp as a lettuce.

So he stood in the bowl of the desert
and sweated.

A drop, which he flicked off his nose
into the sand, sprang up. 'Garlic'

said God, breaking it open;
then handed each man his clove

for planting, till one remained,
which he bit and rubbed round the bowl.

3.
In my mother's house every comfort,
her loving welcome, rotating
meals: meat, vegetables, tinned
fruit and cream.
                    But no garlic.

4.
Though you've moved house
I'm at once at home:
the hallway's strange
but it smells the same.

5.
In prayer aspire to the garlic:
your thoughts, like cloves, attentive
to inwardness, expansive

and, as they fatten, flattening
against their crescent neighbours,
accommodating, shaping

one another. A huddled
conspiracy, a concentration
of cloves waiting to hear
how best to savour the world.

6.
Of all her gifts he savoured most
her reticence, her pungent wit,
both attributes he'd hardly known
　　　　　that she possessed.

Though seeing her tenderly withdraw
layer after thin layer of skin
from a garlic clove the night they met
　　　　　he might have guessed.

7.
My first time bursting too fast,
too forcefully, into the chamber,
I remember the disappointment:

Was that it then, that slither of spilled
seed still obscured and enclosed,
like the odour, in purple sheaths?

But now it's different, each time
a pleasure prised slowly apart
so gently it almost hurts

or twisted hard, quick, like last night,
the cloves taken by surprise,
rocking on their backs in delight.

8.
In the dazzle of birdsong this morning
exposed on the tilt of the table—
the green beaks of the garlic
crying out to be planted.

9.
Now every time having to choose:
never again not to notice
my hand selecting some clove.

The poem still growing.